W9-BQT-540

NBA BASKETBALL BASICS

MARK VANCIL

STERLING PUBLISHING CO., INC.
NEW YORK

Title page: **Charles Oakley of the New York Knicks gives out some free pointers.**

Designed by Judy Morgan

All photographs are from NBA Photos; credits are found on page 126

Cover design by Barry Gottlieb, NBA Properties, Inc.

Library of Congress Cataloging-in-Publication Data

Vancil, Mark, [date]
    NBA basketball basics / by Mark Vancil
        p.   cm.
    Includes index.
    ISBN 0-8069-0927-7
    1. Basketball—United States—Juvenile literature.   [1. Basketball.]
  I. National Basketball Association.   II. Title.
    GV885.1.V36   1995
    796.323'0973—dc20   94-44687
                                                        CIP
                                                         AC

10 9 8 7 6 5 4 3 2

First paperback edition published in 1995 by
Sterling Publishing Company, Inc.
387 Park Avenue South, New York, N.Y. 10016
© 1995 by Mark NBA Properties, Inc.
Distributed in Canada by Sterling Publishing
% Canadian Manda Group, One Atlantic Avenue, Suite 105
Toronto, Ontario, Canada M6K 3E7
Distributed in Great Britain and Europe by Cassell PLC
Wellington House, 125 Strand, London WC2R 0BB, England
Distributed in Australia by Capricorn Link (Australia) Pty Ltd.
P.O. Box 6651, Baulkham Hills, Business Centre, NSW 2153, Australia
Printed and bound in Hong Kong
All rights reserved

Sterling ISBN 0-8069-0927-7   Trade
                      0-8069-0928-5   Paper

Contents

introduction

no sport moves more quickly or requires as many skills as basketball. On defense, a blocked shot or a steal can lead to a fast-break basket at the other end of the court.

On offense, one quick move can result in an easy basket. Good dribbling and passing skills can set up wide-open shots for teammates. And at the NBA level, the best long-range shooters can step behind the three-point line and confound defenses with three-point baskets.

But long before players become part of the excitement on the court, they must first learn and study the basics. This takes a great deal of practice and attention to detail. The basic skills of dribbling, passing and shooting are essential to the continued improvement of every basketball player at every level.

Before Michael Jordan could fly through the air and slam dunk he had to learn how to dribble. Magic Johnson had to learn the basic one- and two-handed passes before he could make "no look" passes to teammates. And Larry Bird first had to master short-range shots before he became a great three-point shooter.

Ballhandling, or dribbling, is a key skill every player must possess. It takes a great deal of practice to be able to dribble effectively with either hand. Players should be able to dribble the ball with their shooting hand while moving without losing control of the ball. A player with the ball must dribble to move around the court and toward the basket. Once the player stops dribbling, he cannot start dribbling again unless the ball is knocked out of his hands by a defensive player. He must pass or shoot.

The last basic skill required to play the game of basketball is shooting. It takes a lot of practice to master the finer points of shooting, and all players should understand the mechanics involved in shooting a shot. Although younger players might need two hands to shoot the ball at first, everyone should learn to shoot the ball with one hand while using the other as a guide.

Since basketball requires much movement, players must be able to run. You don't necessarily have to run fast, but you must be comfortable moving side to side and up and down the court.

Opposite: **Utah Jazz power forward Karl Malone takes aim from the free-throw line.**

When Orlando Magic superstar Shaquille O'Neal walks into the lockerroom, his game gear is already in place. Like anyone else playing serious basketball, O'Neal's uniform includes all the basics.

They are the same in every NBA lockerroom for every professional player. They should be the same for you as well. Since the game relies on the feet, it's best to wear shoes made specifically for basketball. Because there are so many twists and turns, good shoes are important to help guard against injury.

Players should wear at least one pair of white athletic socks. They help guard against blisters that can form when your feet rub against the inside of the shoes. It's equally important to make sure the shoes are tied snugly. They shouldn't be tied too tight or left too loose.

Some players choose to wear wrist bands. These are usually placed just above the wrist and are designed to keep sweat from running down onto a player's hand and making the ball difficult to handle. Other players also wear knee pads. Patrick Ewing is one player who prefers to play with knee pads. In Ewing's case, the pads provide protection against banging knees with another player, which can be painful. Most players, however, prefer to play without pads on their knees.

Once dressed, players head out onto the court. Before actually doing any shooting or running, they always do some warm-ups, and you should also. The usual routine includes light running or jogging in place followed by stretching of the legs and back. Stretching is important to guard against muscle strain and injury. It also helps get blood flowing through the muscles, which in turn allows players to be more flexible.

**Houston Rockets Center
Hakeem Olajuwon scores
with a two-handed dunk.**

Houston Rockets center Hakeem Olajuwon stretches before the start of another game.

Sitting on the floor with legs spread apart, reach the left hand to the toes of the right foot. Make sure the movements are slow and not a bouncing motion. Repeat on the other side with the right hand reaching out and touching the left toes. Make sure to keep your legs straight. This is just one quick stretching drill. There are a number of other stretches covered later in the book.

An NBA basketball court is 94 feet long and 50 feet across. Courts are divided exactly in half. The offensive team has 10 seconds to move the ball over the half-court line following a basket, missed shot or turnover by the opposition. At every level the rim of the basket is exactly 10 feet off the ground. The basket hangs over the lane, which is the painted area running from the end line to the free-throw line. This area is 16 feet wide in the NBA. The distance from the free-throw line to the basket is exactly 15 feet. So when an announcer

You should warm up
also, before practice
or play.

Remember to
stretch slowly to
guard against
injury.

says a player hit a "15-foot jump shot," that means he made the shot from the same distance as a free throw.

> **Key rule:** No part of an offensive player can be in the "lane" for more than three seconds at a time. If an offensive player has even part of one foot in the lane for more than three seconds, referees can call a three-second violation and turn the ball over to the defending team. There are no restrictions, however, on how long defensive players can be in the lane.

The other important line on a basketball court is the three-point line. It runs from one side of the basket across the court in a semi-circle. When a player makes a basket from beyond that line it counts three points instead of two. All other baskets count as two points. Free throws count as one point each.

However, players must be behind the three-point line to be awarded three points. If even a toe is on the line, the shot counts as two points. At youth levels, grade school for example, there usually isn't a three-point line. In high school, the three-point line is 19 feet, 9 inches from the basket. In college the line is also 19 feet, 9 inches, and in the NBA the line is 22 feet from the basket.

Once dressed, warmed up and familiar with the court, players need basic skills to get started. The following chapters will show you the fundamentals required to improve your skills. But remember: only practice makes better players.

ballhandling

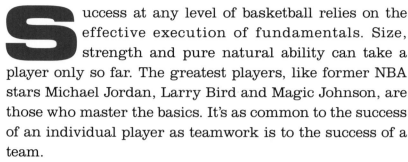

Overleaf: **Phoenix Suns point guard Kevin Johnson attempts to dribble past a defender.**

Success at any level of basketball relies on the effective execution of fundamentals. Size, strength and pure natural ability can take a player only so far. The greatest players, like former NBA stars Michael Jordan, Larry Bird and Magic Johnson, are those who master the basics. It's as common to the success of an individual player as teamwork is to the success of a team.

One of the most basic building blocks in a player's development is ballhandling, or dribbling. For smaller players, dribbling skills are essential to move around bigger players and create scoring opportunities. For taller players, ballhandling skills can be the difference between becoming a very good player and an excellent one.

Having effective ballhandlers is also a key for any team offense. Solid ballhandlers are needed to run the fast break, set up the offense and avoid the defense. In other words, whether big or small, fast or slow, every player must develop ballhandling skills.

There are five basic dribbles players should practice and learn to master. In each you should always control the ball with your fingers. Do not use the palm of your hand. Spread your fingers comfortably and use them to control the ball. You should learn to dribble the ball with either hand without looking at it. Ideally, the ball should bounce no higher than your waist when it comes back up off the floor. Bend over a little and keep your knees bent slightly.

1. CONTROL DRIBBLE This dribble is used when a player is guarded closely by a defensive player. You should keep your body between the defender and the ball. Bounce the ball slightly away from your body. That makes it much more difficult for a defender to knock the ball away. Use your off hand, or the hand you are not using to dribble, to further protect the ball.

By keeping your head up and your eyes off the ball, you will be able to spot open teammates for a pass or find openings for yourself. This dribble is the most basic of the ballhandling skills.

2. SPEED DRIBBLE This is used most often

Seattle SuperSonics point guard Gary Payton is a master of the speed dribble.

when a player is not being guarded closely. The speed dribble is used on fast breaks, quick drives to the basket or following a steal in the open court. Push the ball out in front of your body when you are dribbling in a full sprint.

The speed dribble allows you to move up and down the court quickly when you are in the open. It is important to develop enough confidence in this skill that you keep your eyes off the ball while dribbling equally well with either hand.

Golden State point guard Tim Hardaway has the quickest crossover dribble in the NBA.

3. SPIN, OR REVERSE, DRIBBLE

The spin, or reverse, dribble allows you to change direction and keep your body between the ball and the defensive player at all times.

If you are dribbling with your right hand and want to switch to the left, the reverse is a perfect option. Simply stop, plant your left foot and spin into the opposite direction with your back to the defender. As you spin, change the dribble from the right hand to the left while keeping the ball close to your body. This move is also referred to as a reverse pivot.

4. CROSSOVER DRIBBLE

Golden State guard Tim Hardaway is considered the master of the crossover dribble, which involves switching the ball from hand to hand while facing your opponent. If you were dribbling to your right, for example, and wanted to make a quick move to the left, you would step back with your left foot and bounce the ball from your right hand to your left. The lower you bounce the ball, the quicker the crossover. Again, guide the ball with your fingertips and do not let it move up into your palm.

Since the defensive player doesn't know where you are headed, the crossover is one of the most effective moves for changing direction to get past a defender. It can also be used to gain better ball protection. More than with any other dribbling skill, quickness is the key to an effective crossover. Every NBA player uses the crossover dribble, particularly when making a move to the basket.

5. CHANGE-OF-PACE DRIBBLE

This dribble is for the more advanced player. Once you have mastered the other four dribbles, the change-of-pace dribble is relatively easy to develop. The idea is simple. Change the pace of your dribble and throw the defensive player off balance. Driving by a defender who is either out of position or off balance is much easier.

For example, dribble at about half speed to your right. When the defensive player adjusts to that pace, speed up and dribble past him. Few defenders can recover, particularly on a drive to the basket when the change-of-pace dribble is executed perfectly. Practice changing the pace from slow to fast and back to slow again.

Muggsy Bogues of the Charlotte Hornets uses the reverse dribble against Washington's Rex Chapman.

individual drills:

walking dribble

Beginners should get comfortable with the ball by dribbling while walking up and down the court. The key to this drill is control. Pick a spot on the wall at the opposite end of the court and dribble toward the spot with your right hand. Keep your head up and your eyes fixed on that spot. On the way back, pick out another spot, only this time dribble with your left hand.

It will take some time to develop both hands. Remember, you must be able to dribble with either hand to be an effective offensive player. After you feel comfortable dribbling in straight lines at a walking speed, try doing the same drill while jogging slowly. Continue to move faster as you become able to go up and down the court without losing control of the ball.

Keep your head up and spend at least as much time with your left hand as your right.

Orlando Magic point guard Anfernee "Penny" Hardaway uses the walking dribble to move upcourt.

ballhandling drill

Stand about three feet from a wall and hold the ball over your head with both hands. Bounce the ball off the wall 10 times with your right hand and then 10 times with your left hand.

This might be difficult at first, but it helps develop the feel you need to handle the ball. Remember, use your finger pads.

reverse spin

Place a chair in front of the free-throw line. Pretend that chair is a defensive player and dribble toward the chair with either hand. If you are dribbling with your right hand, plant your left foot as you approach the chair and spin. Switch the ball to your left hand and continue toward the basket for a layup.

Practice this drill with both hands. The reverse dribble is a highly effective offensive move, especially when you are being guarded closely.

Plant the foot opposite your dribbling hand.

Transfer your dribbling hand as you spin back.

**Dribble around
your opponent . . .**

**. . . and on to the
basket.**

figure-eight ballhandling drill

This is an excellent drill for players of all levels. Bend over slightly with your knees about shoulder width apart and slightly bent. Start with the ball in your right hand and pass the ball between your legs in a figure-eight motion. You will be moving the ball from one hand to another.

Keep your feet planted and start slowly. After you feel comfortable passing the ball through your legs from hand to hand, increase the speed.

After you have mastered the figure eight, try moving the ball around your body in a circle. Start at your ankles and pass the ball around them using both hands. Move up to your knees, then your waist. Again, start slowly and work up in speed.

Move the ball back through your legs . . .

. . . to your other hand. Bring the ball around . . .

. . . and go back
through your legs
the other way.

Work on good con-
trol before speed.

As you near the chair get ready to change direction and hands.

Dribble down from one hand up to the other.

crossover dribble

For more advanced players, there are a number of drills to help develop the crossover dribble.

Place chairs at different spots down the middle of the court or driveway. Dribble toward the chair as if it were a defensive player. As you near the chair quickly change hands and go around it. Do this from right to left and back again, concentrating on moving quickly while maintaining control of the ball.

Remember, keep the ball low as you bounce it from hand to hand. Learn to do this move quickly.

Keep the ball low
and under
control.

Keep the ball
away from the
chair as you
dribble.

Bu**ll**ets ™

one-on-one

Players line up at one end of the court in three or four lines equally spread along the baseline. The first player in each line takes a defensive position while the second player in line takes the ball.

Staying within a 10-foot lane, the player with the ball attempts to dribble upcourt against the defender. Since the player with the ball cannot use the entire court to go around the defender, he is forced to use many of the basic dribbles to get upcourt. The player must use both hands.

When the two players reach the end they switch positions. A key here is to protect the ball from the defensive player while keeping your eyes off the floor.

press breaker

This is a more advanced drill for players who have become comfortable with all the basic dribbles.

Place three to five defensive players at various spots down the court. The player with the ball starts by himself underneath the basket. While the defensive players try to force him into corners or "traps," the offensive player must keep his eyes up and work his way up the court through the defense without picking up his dribble or losing control of the ball.

Make sure you practice with both hands. The best players are able to handle the ball equally well with either hand.

Keep your eyes off the ball and your head up.

Keep the ball on your fingers and out of the palm of your hand.

Try to keep the ball from bouncing above the waist when dribbling.

When guarded closely or making a move toward the basket, try to keep the ball from bouncing above the knees. Control is the key.

passing

good passing is as important to a team's success as scoring or defense. In fact, after ballhandling and shooting, passing might be the most important fundamental in all of basketball.

Why? Because passing is the key to a good offense. A good passer can create easy baskets for his teammates. A team full of good passers can pick apart even the greatest defense. Look at the best teams and you usually find a team that revolves around a great passer.

When the Boston Celtics and Los Angeles Lakers were fighting for NBA championships in the 1980s, the Celtics' Larry Bird and the Lakers' Magic Johnson were known as two of the greatest passers in history. The Detroit Pistons won two NBA titles with Isiah Thomas leading the offense and setting up his teammates with his brilliant passing ability. The Chicago Bulls were a perfect example of a team that had solid passers at all five starting positions.

When you hear someone talk about players who make their teammates better, they are usually referring to players with sharp passing skills. Even Utah Jazz superstar Karl Malone isn't sure what kind of player he would be without the passing of teammate John Stockton.

"I don't want to find out," says Malone.

As with ballhandling and shooting, good passing relies on the proper use of fundamentals. Though there are a number of different passes, all of them involve the same basic elements.

The most important of these is to use your fingertips and not the palm of your hand when passing. Milwaukee Bucks coach Mike Dunleavy was an NBA guard before he turned to coaching and he mastered all the basic passes during the course of his career.

"There are two basic passes every player must learn and be able to use effectively," says Dunleavy. "One is the two-handed chest pass and the other is the two-handed bounce pass. The fundamentals are the same with each. You have to keep the ball on your fingertips."

Probably the best place to hold the ball before dribbling, passing or taking a shot is right around the chest with both hands. Dunleavy calls it the "triple threat position."

Opposite: **Former Boston Celtics star Larry Bird throws a two-handed overhead pass to a teammate.**

Utah Jazz point guard John Stockton is considered one of the greatest passers in league history.

Once you're in the "triple threat position," you can dribble, pass or shoot.

New Jersey Nets power forward Derrick Coleman throws a two-handed chest pass.

"When you are holding the ball with both hands in that position there isn't anything you can't do," says Dunleavy. "You can put the ball on the floor and dribble past the defender, go up for a jump shot if the defender drops off or throw a pass. And, from that position you can fake any of those moves before you actually make a move or a pass."

Cleveland Cavaliers point guard Mark Price fires a one-handed pass to a teammate.

THE TWO-HANDED CHEST PASS

Spread the fingers of each hand on either side of the ball. Push the ball out from your chest, fully extending your arms. Snap your wrists outward so that the back of your hands are facing one another. By snapping your wrists outward you will get rotation, or backspin, on the ball, which makes the pass easier to control for you and your teammate on the receiving end. Remember to follow through with the palms away from the body.

THE TWO-HANDED BOUNCE PASS

On a bounce pass, follow the same motion. The only difference is that you should locate a spot on the floor about three quarters of the way between you and your teammate. Try to hit that spot on the bounce.

"To make the pass even more accurate, step toward the spot or the player you are throwing the ball to," says Dunleavy. "The bounce pass should hit your teammate about waist high. You do not want to throw a pass that bounces below the knees or over the waist. A pass too low is difficult to handle, while a pass that bounces too high is easy to steal."

THE TWO-HANDED OVERHEAD PASS

This pass is used most often by centers or taller players at the start of a fast break. But it can be an effective pass for every player regardless of size. Not only does it allow you to keep the ball away from the defensive player, but it's easy to control. Again, the same fundamentals should be applied to this pass. Hold the ball over your head with both hands, then bring both hands out and down, snapping your wrists just as you would on the chest pass.

To improve accuracy, take a small step in the direction you are making the pass. Be sure to follow through and snap the wrists outward.

For the more advanced players, there are a number of other passes that can be used during the course of a game. You should work on all of them after getting comfortable with the two-handed chest, bounce and overhead passes.

The two-handed chest pass . . .

. . . starts with the fingers spread on both hands.

Push the ball fully out from your chest and . . .

follow through by snapping your wrists with your palms out.

OFF-THE-DRIBBLE PASS

OFF-THE-DRIBBLE PASS John Stockton might be the best player in the world at this pass.

Instead of bouncing the ball back down toward the floor for another dribble, Stockton brings his hand behind the ball, and instead of pushing the ball back to the floor, he pushes it forward in the form of a pass to a teammate.

This may be the quickest pass in basketball because there is really no set-up involved. It's also very difficult for defensive players to steal since they are usually expecting the passer to take another dribble.

John Stockton of the Utah Jazz is ready to make an off-the-dribble pass.

Phoenix Suns forward Charles Barkley prepares to fire a baseball pass downcourt.

BASEBALL PASS   The baseball pass is used primarily for long passes. Bring the ball behind your head just past your ear. Don't bring the ball too far back. To control the pass, you have to keep it close to your head. The motion is similar to that of a baseball catcher throwing a ball to second base. Follow through just as you would with a baseball. As you follow through, snap your wrist straight down.

The two-handed pass is a powerful weapon for Milwaukee Bucks point guard Eric Murdock.

If your wrist twists to the right or left, then the pass will do the same. Snapping the wrist straight down cuts down on the "curve ball" effect, as Dunleavy calls it.

BEHIND-THE-BACK PASS Although some consider this a "fancy" pass, many players use the behind-the-back pass with great results. It can be thrown either off the dribble, standing still or while moving toward the basket. When done properly, the behind-the-back pass is very difficult to defend against.

To practice this pass stand sideways with your feet parallel. Bring the ball around your back with your right hand behind and slightly below the ball. As always, follow through completely. Practice this pass often with each hand before attempting to use it in a game.

LOB OR ALLEY-OOP PASS This is a very difficult pass to perfect.

Though the pass is used often at the college and NBA level, it takes near-perfect timing to complete. The pass usually is thrown to a player either running down the floor or preparing to jump high into the air near the basket. It can also be used when trying to throw over the top of a defender guarding a teammate too closely.

In the NBA, a typical lob pass is thrown off the dribble high into the air toward the basket. The timing has to be perfect since the player receiving the pass is usually timing his jump so he can catch the ball and either lay it in the basket or dunk it all in one motion.

On a fast break, the lob can be used to "lead" a player running ahead of the defense. This too involves perfect timing. Ideally the pass should be thrown softly with an arc so the teammate can run underneath the pass and catch it in stride on the way to the basket.

Seattle SuperSonics forward Shawn Kemp receives an alley-oop and dunks it.

individual drills

target drill

This is one of the few passing drills players can work on by themselves.

Pick out at least three spots on a wall at different heights. Start about 10 feet from the wall and practice the two-handed chest pass, the two-handed bounce pass and the two-handed overhead pass.

Try to imagine yourself in a game throwing these passes to a teammate. Concentrate on hitting the spot every time. Throw at least 10 passes at each of the three targets. After the first set, move back five feet and do another set. Do this until you are 20 feet from the wall.

Try to hit the same spot on the wall . . ,

. . . with each of the two-handed passes . . .

. . . at least 10 times for each pass.

line passing

Make two lines with the first player in each line facing the first player in the other line. The lines should be 10 to 12 feet apart to start.

The first player in Line 1 makes a two-handed chest pass to the first player in Line 2. After the pass the player in Line 1 runs to the end of Line 2. As he does, the player who received the pass makes a two-handed chest pass to the next player in the opposite line. Following the pass he also moves to the end of the opposite line.

Go through this drill until every player has thrown a pass from the first distance. Then move back 8 to 10 feet and repeat. Do the same thing after moving back another 8 to 10 feet.

After completing all three distances with the chest pass, do the same routine with a two-handed bounce pass and two-handed overhead pass.

Key rule: Players cannot take more than one and a half steps with the ball without passing to another player. Taking more than one and a half steps is called "traveling" and results in the ball being turned over to the other team.

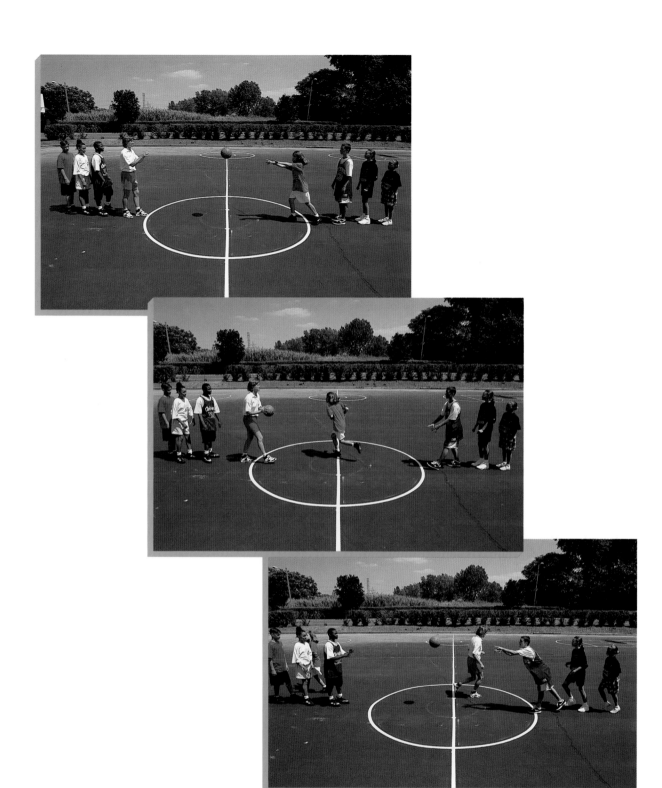

three-man weave

Start with three lines of players spread evenly across one end of the court. The middle player takes the ball and passes to the player on the right, who crosses to the center. As he does, the middle player runs behind that player to the right and continues downcourt.

The player who started on the right then passes across to the player on the left, who has now crossed to the center slightly in front of him. He then runs behind the player on the left and continues downcourt. The player who started on the left is now in the middle and starts the passing drill all over again as the three players move downcourt.

The ball should not hit the ground. As the three players head toward the basket, the last player receiving the pass goes in for a layup and continues up the right or left side of the court. The weave starts all over again with another layup ending the drill for the first three players at the other end of the court.

The next three players then take over.

To make the drill a little more fun, try to make 21 straight "weaves" up and down the court without throwing the ball away or missing one of the layups. This also works as a conditioning exercise.

FAST-BREAK DRILL   This is another combination ballhandling, passing and conditioning drill.

One line forms under one basket with another line either to the right or left of the free-throw line extending toward the sideline. A shot is taken either by the coach or another player. The first two players in line under the basket get in rebounding position. The player who rebounds the pass throws a two-handed overhead pass to the first player out near the free-throw line and runs behind him on his way downcourt. The other player fills the opposite lane, while the player receiving the pass dribbles down the middle of the court.

The player with the ball stops at the free-throw line and throws a two-handed bounce pass to one of the two players coming down the sides for a layup.

The drill goes until all players are at the other end of the court. Then the drill starts over.

The player coming to the middle from the left gets the ball from the player in the middle who crosses left behind him.

The player who started on the left passes to the player on the right.

The player who started on the right crosses to the middle and passes . . .

. . . to the player now on the left who comes back to the middle to pass or shoot.

Keep the ball on your fingertips and out of your palms.

Follow through on all passes.

On two-handed chest and bounce passes, snap your wrists out at the end of the passing motion.

To increase accuracy take a small step toward the teammate you are passing to.

Passes should be sharp and crisp and delivered so that they can be easily handled by teammates on the receiving end.

shooting

according to Dunleavy, all shooting starts with a basic set-up. By getting into the proper position to shoot, your aim is improved and you are better able to shoot from longer distances.

THE BASIC SET-UP "The basic set-up is very important before you shoot," says Dunleavy, who was a fine shooting guard for a number of NBA teams including the Bucks. "The first thing you have to do is get your body square to the basket. Getting your body square sets up the rest of the shooting process. By square I mean you must have good balance with equal weight on each foot.

"If you are a right-handed shooter, you want to have your right foot slightly in front of the left. If you are a left-handed shooter, put your left foot slightly ahead of the right. Either way, don't have the lead foot more than five inches in front of the back foot."

That is the basic set-up for your legs and feet. To make sure that you are in the proper set-up, Dunleavy has an easy test to check your balance. Set up as if you were ready to shoot and have a teammate push your chest with one or two fingers. If you fall backward, your feet are too close together. But if one foot is slightly in front of the other, you won't fall back. Why is balance so important to shooting? Simple. All power to shoot comes not from your arms but from your legs.

"Once your feet are balanced, stick your butt out and put your head out over the ball," advises Dunleavy.

To get your "guidance system" in order, hold your arm out and put the ball in the palm of your hand. After you get comfortable holding the ball, turn the ball up like a waiter carrying a tray. Balance the ball in your fingers and hold it to one side of your head slightly off the shoulder.

SHOOTING THE BALL Now practice shooting the ball with one hand from that position. Make sure you are close to the basket. Push the ball straight until your arm extends completely and your elbow locks. Follow through by snapping the wrist in a downward waving motion. By

Overleaf: **Golden State's Chris Mullin is one of the best shooters in basketball.**

keeping your elbow in line with your body the ball has to go straight up and out.

It is very important to shoot the ball with your fingers. As you snap your wrists on the follow-through, the ball should roll off your fingertips. That will produce good backspin on the ball. Your middle finger usually has the last contact with it.

Do not shoot with the ball in the palm of your hand. Also, keep your elbow in close to your body. Do not shoot with your elbow facing away from your body.

As you become more comfortable shooting with one hand from a set position, you too will begin to bring the ball up into a natural shooting position with both hands whether off the dribble or after receiving a pass from a teammate.

"You want to keep that follow-through the same way every time," says Dunleavy. "It should be the same on every shot. And lock in on your target with your eyes. I used to look at the back of the rim and really concentrate on that target. Some players like to concentrate on the front of the rim and others on the whole basket. Whatever you choose, lock in on that spot.

"When you're ready to shoot, use your other hand as a guide. Remember, it's only there for set-up and balance. You are not trying to shoot with both hands. If the off hand is too far in front of the ball or too far behind, it will be much more difficult to keep the shot going straight toward the basket. Practice each of these steps until it becomes routine."

shots for shooters

BANK SHOT   The square on the front of a backboard can provide an assist for players who know how to use it. When shooting a shot from either side of the basket, whether layup, set shot or jump shot, it is always easier to use the backboard to deflect the shot into the basket.

Use the square as a guide when trying to make a bank shot. Let's say you are standing 10 feet from the basket on the right side in between the corner and the free-throw line. Using proper form, aim the shot inside the square on the

right side of the basket. If you apply proper form and shoot the ball off the square, it is much more likely to go in.

Make sure you have the same arc you would use on a regular shot. The only difference is that instead of shooting at the basket you are shooting at the square. As you become more comfortable using the bank shot, you will learn how to measure the shots and where to aim inside the square.

LAYUP   This is one of the easiest shots in basketball, but it is also an important one to master. As with other shots, form is extremely important.

If you are right-handed, dribble the ball toward the basket from the right side. As you approach the basket, bring your right leg, hand and arm up at the same time while pushing off your left foot and jumping into the air.

Your right arm and leg should go up at approximately the same time. Shoot the ball with your right hand up off the backboard, banking it into the basket. Remember to follow through.

Chicago Bulls forward Scottie Pippen uses perfect form to complete this layup.

For a right-handed layup, dribble in from the right.

Pull your right leg up as you load your right hand.

Jump off your left leg, extending your right leg and arm at the same time.

Aim your shot to bank off the backboard and follow through.

SET SHOT   A set shot is exactly what it sounds like. A player sets himself before he shoots. Instead of jumping into the air and trying to get up and over a defender before releasing the ball, a player sets himself, bends his knees only slightly and pushes off the floor as he pushes the shot toward the basket.

Few NBA players shoot the ball as well as Indiana Pacers guard Reggie Miller.

The set shot begins with the basic set-up—square to the basket, knees bent, ball on your fingertips in the waiter's position, elbow in line with your body.

Push off the court with your feet, don't jump, as you aim the shot. Power in the shot comes from your legs, control from your arms.

Push your arm straight out until your elbow locks and follow through by snapping your wrist down to produce good backspin.

Former Boston great Larry Bird had an almost perfect delivery on his jump shot.

JUMP SHOT The most common shot at the higher levels of basketball, particularly in the NBA, is the jump shot. The shot involves jumping straight up into the air, bringing the ball up to the shooting position with both hands and shooting the ball at the top of the jump. For advanced players, mastering the jump shot is one of the most important skills in basketball.

Cleveland's Mark Price makes up for his lack of size with a deadly jump shot.

No player has ever used the hook shot as effectively as Hall of Fame center Kareem Abdul-Jabbar.

HOOK SHOT

Former NBA superstar Kareem Abdul-Jabbar had one of the greatest hook shots in history. This shot is especially effective around the basket against taller players.

Like a layup, the right leg goes up with the right arm for a right-handed player. Instead of facing the basket, however, turn your body slightly to the side. Bring the ball out, up and over your head in a sweeping motion. Push off your left foot, extend your arm high over your head and flip the ball toward the basket, either through the net, or off the backboard. Remember to follow through.

This shot is effective when you are guarded by another player close to the basket. Although Abdul-Jabbar could make hook shots from nearly 15 feet away, most young players will want to start out shooting the hook from no more than five feet.

DUNK   This is the only shot that usually demands size, strength and jumping ability, although size is not necessarily vital. Michael Jordan, Dominique Wilkins and even 5-foot 7-inch Spud Webb have been among some of the NBA's greatest dunkers.

Instead of laying the ball over the rim or banking it off the backboard, these players can jump high enough to get the ball up and over the rim while it is still in their hand. Once over the rim they dunk, or slam, the ball through the net. This can be done with one or two hands.

Key rule: It is illegal at every level, however, to hang on to the rim after a dunk. This is a matter of safety.

Chicago Bulls superstar Michael Jordan goes up for one of his famous dunks.

individual drills

Hold the ball in the waiter's position.

one-hand drill

Practice shooting the ball with only one hand. Hold the ball in the "waiter's position," as Dunleavy calls it, and stand close enough to the basket so that you are able to use good form.

Beginners should start about five feet from the basket, either in front of it or to the side. By using only your shooting hand, you will be forced to shoot straight. Again, practice from short range so you become comfortable with proper form. Once you start making these shots, take one step back and continue to practice.

Bend your knees, arch your back.

Don't forget to follow through.

chair shooting

Another great drill to develop proper form begins by placing a chair about five feet in front of the basket. Again, practice shooting the ball with one hand. By sitting down in the chair you will be forced to fully extend your arm and follow through with a snap of the wrist. If you shoot the ball flat, or fail to use the proper technique, the ball won't make it over the rim and it certainly won't go straight.

flat back

This is a good drill for beginners. Lie down on your back and practice shooting the ball straight up into the air. The ball should come straight down. If it goes to one side or the other, check your guide hand. Make sure you are extending straight up and snapping your wrist in the downward wave.

spot shooting

Move around the free-throw lane taking shots from seven different spots. Do not move until you have made a shot from that spot.

Start just to the right of the basket on the free-throw lane. Next, move halfway between the end line and the free-throw line. Go to the corner of the free-throw line, the middle, the opposite corner of the free-throw line and then work your way back down the other side of the lane.

spot shooting for advanced players

The spot drill is an excellent combination workout/shooting drill when done individually. Take shots from the same spots, but only one at a time. In between, run down the ball and dribble back out to the next spot. Pretend you are either receiving a pass from a teammate or setting yourself up for an open shot off the dribble.

Continue working around the perimeter until you have taken 50 shots, 10 at each of the five spots. Again, concentrate on form and footwork. Take the shots quickly, as if you were playing in a live game.

team spot shooting

Put one player under the basket to rebound. The shooter moves around the court to each of five spots. Starting in the corner, he takes five shots with the rebounder passing him the ball. Beginners should start near the end line no more than 10 to 12 feet from the basket, intermediate players 12 to 15 feet and high school players 15 to 18 feet from the basket.

After taking five shots from the corner, the shooter moves to a spot between the corner and the free-throw circle, keeping the same distance from the basket. After five shots, the shooter moves to the free-throw line, to a spot between the free-throw circle and the opposite corner and then to the corner. Take five shots at each spot, then go back around. Be sure to concentrate on your form, but also try to move quickly.

After 50 shots, the shooter and rebounder switch.

team shooting game

Divide the team into two groups, one at each end of the court.

The two teams line up at 15 to 18 feet from the basket on one side. At the sound of the whistle, players from both teams start shooting, one at a time. When a player makes a shot from the corner, the whole team moves to a spot the same distance from the basket between the corner and the free-throw line. As soon as somebody makes that shot, everyone moves to the free-throw line and then back down the opposite side.

The winning team is the team that can go around and back first by hitting shots at all 10 spots.

team drills

Set up with one foot a little in front of the other.

Bend your knees slightly.

The ball should be in the "waiter's" position on your fingertips and not in the palm of your hand.

Follow through by extending your elbow and snapping the wrist, which allows the ball to roll off your fingers, creating good backspin.

Keep your other hand to the side of the ball as a guide only.

Let the ball come off of your fingertips.

Use your legs.

mike dunleavy's shooting tips

Chris Mullin of Golden State releases a jump shot.

shooting games

H·O·R·S·E   This game might be the most popular shooting game of all time. It can be played with two or more players and one ball.

Player A starts the game by taking a shot from anywhere on the court. The next player, or players, then goes to that exact spot and shoots. Every player who misses gets a letter. So if Player A makes a shot from the free-throw line and Player B misses, then Player B has an "H". The same with Player C, and so on.

Player A has the right to shoot from anywhere on the court as long as he makes his shot. When Player A misses, then Player B is allowed to establish the shot by shooting from any spot on the floor. If Player B makes a 10-foot shot, for example, then every other player must make the shot, including Player A.

If Player B misses the shot, assuming there are more than two players in the game, then Player C gets the right to shoot from anywhere on the court. The process continues until one player gets all five letters, or H-O-R-S-E.

If only two players are in the game, the process is the same. Player A has "honors" until he misses. When he does miss, Player B takes over the shooting. Player A is then forced to follow and risk earning a letter.

Note: You only earn a letter when you miss a shot that has been established. If you are the first player in the game, or if you gain honors during the course of the game, you do not earn a letter for missing a shot. Only when you miss a shot that another player has established, do you gain a letter.

Want to play a shorter version of the game? How about P-I-G?

KNOCKOUT   This is one of Dunleavy's favorites. Any number of players can compete, although four or five at a time is desirable.

Much like a game of H-O-R-S-E, one player takes a shot from any spot on the floor and all the other players must follow if the shot is established. A free throw counts as one point, a regular shot as two points and anything beyond the three-point line counts as three points.

The idea is to get 21 points as fast as possible. As players reach 21 they leave the game. The last player left is the loser. Since he is an excellent three-point shooter, you can see why Dunleavy is tough to beat at this game.

AROUND THE WORLD   Two or more players move around the "lane" at seven different spots.

Player A starts the game by standing just to the right of the basket on the lane. If he makes his shot, then he moves midway up to the free-throw line. After making that shot the next one is taken from the corner of the free-throw line, then the middle of the free-throw line, the opposite corner of the free-throw line, midway down the opposite side of the lane and finally just to the left of the basket.

You only move after you have made a shot at a given stop. The winner is the player who gets all the way "around the world" the quickest. Remember, no one moves to the next spot until he has made his shot. Players alternate shots, so one player could get stuck on one spot the entire game.

21   It's best to play 21 with three players, although the game can handle as many as five.

In a three-man game of 21, two players start out under the basket in rebounding position. Another player goes to the free-throw line and shoots up to three free throws. The offensive player shoots the free throws, until he misses or makes three shots. Each shot he makes counts as one point.

If he makes all three free throws, then that player takes the ball from the top of the key, or the arc above the free-throw line, and tries to score on the two defenders. He can drive, shoot a jump shot, throw up a hook or do whatever it takes to make a basket. The usual rules apply to the defensive players, meaning that they can't foul.

If the offensive player makes the shot, which counts as two points, then he returns to the free-throw line and shoots up to three more free throws.

If he misses a free throw, either at the beginning of the

game or after making a basket, then the ball is live. That means anyone can grab the rebound and try to put it into the basket. So if Player A misses a free throw and Player B rebounds and scores, then Player B goes to the line for up to three free throws.

The object of the game is to see which player can accumulate 21 points first.

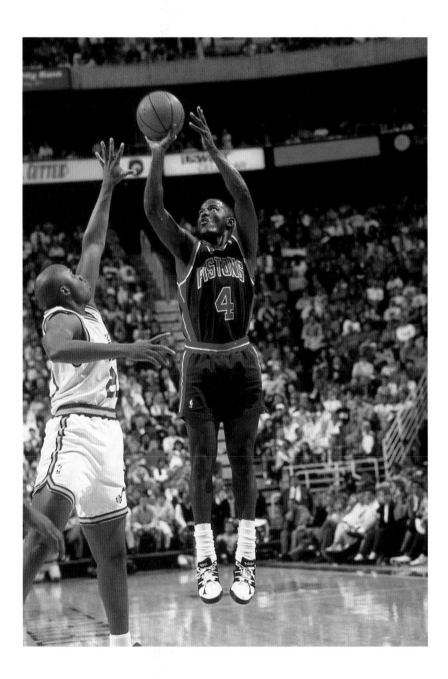

Joe Dumars of the Detroit Pistons is always a scoring threat.

positions

the five basic positions on a basketball team are the same at every level. A starting team consists of two guards, two forwards and a center.

During the course of a game, however, it's possible that teams, particularly at the NBA level, would change that basic lineup. Depending upon the size and speed of the opponents, NBA teams sometimes use three forwards instead of a center and two forwards. Other teams, the Chicago Bulls for example, often use what they call a "three-guard offense," which consists of three guards and either two forwards or one forward and a center.

While most lineups are fundamentally the same, the duties and demands of each position are different. For example, there can be two guards and two forwards but each of the four players has different roles.

Opposite: **San Antonio's David Robinson is one of the NBA's best centers.**

the numbers game

Maybe you have heard a coach or announcer refer to certain players by a number.

Ever hear Scottie Pippen referred to as a "three" or Mark Price called a "one"? As in baseball, the positions on a basketball team have numbers. Coaches sometimes use these numbers instead of names when designing plays. Announcers use the numbers to show the difference between a small forward and a power forward.

To end the confusion, here are the numbers and the positions they describe:

1—Point Guard   2—Shooting Guard   3—Small Forward   4—Power Forward   5—Center

POSITION 1—POINT GUARD   One guard is usually referred to as a point guard or lead guard. Some of the best NBA point guards are John Stockton of the Utah Jazz, Kevin Johnson of the Phoenix Suns, Gary Payton of the Seattle SuperSonics, Tim Hardaway of the Golden State Warriors, Mark Price of the Cleveland Cavaliers and Kenny Anderson of the New Jersey Nets.

Point guard Gary Payton of the Seattle SuperSonics has to be an excellent ballhandler.

The point guard is extremely important to the success of any team. He often acts like a football quarterback, calling plays and directing the offense. That player is usually the team's best dribbler and passer. It is his duty to bring the ball up the court and set up the plays. Very few teams win championships without a solid point guard able to direct the offense while making few mistakes.

POSITION 2—SHOOTING GUARD The other guard, particularly in the lower levels, has similar duties. But he usually doesn't bring the ball up the court. In the NBA, that player is referred to as a shooting guard, a "two" guard or an "off" guard and is usually bigger than the point guard.

Michael Jordan was one of the greatest shooting guards in history when he played for the Chicago Bulls. Reggie Miller of the Indiana Pacers, Jimmy Jackson of the Dallas

Mavericks, Dan Majerle of the Phoenix Suns, Latrell Sprewell of the Golden State Warriors and Joe Dumars of the Detroit Pistons are some of the best shooting guards in the NBA right now.

While they don't set up the offense or handle the ball as much as the point guard, players like Dumars, Jackson and Sprewell can play either guard spot effectively. The biggest difference between a point guard and a shooting guard is that the shooting guard usually is one of the team's best scorers. Often he takes more shots than the point guard and

Golden State's Latrell Sprewell has become a great all-around shooting guard.

Denver's LaPhonso Ellis is among the NBA's best rebounding power forwards.

is counted on to provide his team with outside, or long-range, shooting.

Players like Johnson and Price combine the skills of both guard positions, which makes them particularly dangerous to opposing defenses.

POSITION 4—POWER FORWARD In the NBA, there are also clear differences at the forward spots. Power forwards, or big forwards as they are sometimes called, are players like New York's Charles Oakley, Utah's Karl Malone, Orlando's Horace Grant, Houston's Otis Thorpe, Charlotte's Larry Johnson, Phoenix's Charles Barkley and Denver's LaPhonso Ellis.

They are known for their size, defense and rebounding. Barkley, Johnson and Malone are three of the few power forwards who rank among the league's top scorers. Most power forwards, especially players like Oakley, Grant and Thorpe, focus on defense and rebounding.

At all levels, these players are usually slightly bigger and stronger than other players. In the NBA they also tend to be a team's best rebounder and one of its best defenders. San Antonio's Dennis Rodman is a perfect example of an NBA power forward who concentrates on those two areas.

POSITION 3—SMALL FORWARD The player opposite a team's power forward is called a small forward. Though they are usually anything but small, Chicago's Scottie Pippen, Phoenix's Danny Manning, Boston's Dominique Wilkins and Dallas's Jamal Mashburn are some of the finest small forwards in the league.

They are known primarily for their ballhandling and scoring ability. Pippen is rather unique in that he's one of the most versatile players in the league. He can play every position on the floor except center.

In the NBA and in college, the small forward is usually one of the most talented players on the floor.

POSITION 5—CENTER Guards and forwards revolve around the center. The center position is very important to a team's offense and defense. That player is

Dallas Mavericks small forward Jamal Mashburn is known for ballhandling and scoring.

usually the tallest player on the team. New York's Patrick Ewing, San Antonio's David Robinson, Houston's Hakeem Olajuwon, Charlotte's Alonzo Mourning and Orlando's Shaquille O'Neal are five of the greatest centers in the NBA.

On offense, players like Ewing, Robinson, Olajuwon and O'Neal are the focus of their respective teams. Their team's offense revolves around them. That's why all four players lead their teams in scoring. In fact, during the 1993/94 season, Robinson, O'Neal and Olajuwon finished as the

NBA's top three scorers, the first time in history three centers occupied the top three spots.

Centers are just as important at the defensive end. Not only must they defend the opposing center, but they are also relied upon to block shots and rebound.

Houston Rockets center Hakeem Olajuwon battles for position with San Antonio's David Robinson.

THE SIXTH MAN

THE SIXTH MAN   Some of the most overlooked players are substitutes. These are the players who start the game on the bench but are called upon when the coach wants to replace one of the starters during the course of a game.

The main substitute or reserve is called the "sixth man." This player has a key role in the success of any team. He is usually the first player off the bench when one of the five starters comes out of the game.

That player is either capable of playing a variety of positions or he is particularly good at one thing. The NBA's best sixth men during the 1993/94 season were Charlotte's Dell Curry, Seattle's Nate McMillan and Atlanta's Craig Ehlo. In Curry's case, he was the NBA's best long-range shooter off the bench. Curry's shooting ability provided the Hornets with an offensive punch when he came into games, which is why he was voted Sixth Man of the Year.

McMillan and Ehlo provide a variety of services for their teams. Both can play solid defense and move between two or three positions. Their versatility makes them valuable as sixth men.

Charlotte Hornets guard Dell Curry won the NBA's Sixth Man Award for the 1993–94 season.

Key rule: The line that divides the court in half is known as the half-court line or the 10-second line. When moving from one end of the court toward your basket, your team has 10 seconds to get the ball across the half-court line.

plays

there are hundreds of plays designed to result in baskets for the offensive team. There are just as many defensive alignments designed to stop offensive players from scoring those points.

But there are two offensive moves, or plays, all players should learn. In one way or another, they are part of virtually every offense ever created. Both are designed to help the offensive player break free of a tough defense for an open shot.

THE PICK AND ROLL The first play is called a "pick and roll." The pick and roll involves two offensive players working together, one of whom has the ball. The play can be executed by any two of the five players on the court. It can also be used anywhere on the court and is highly effective against defenders playing very close to offensive players.

The player dribbling the ball heads in the direction of a teammate. Since the defensive player is focused on the dribbler, he might not see the other offensive player behind him. As the dribbler continues in the direction of his teammate, the teammate stops with the middle of his chest lined up opposite the shoulder of the defender. When setting up, the player should stand with knees slightly bent, arms down at the side and feet parallel.

Opposite: **Houston Rockets' Kenny Smith drives Utah Jazz' John Stockton into a pick set by Hakeem Olajuwon.**

> **Key rule:** The second player, or teammate, must give the defensive player at least one step before he sets up.

The player dribbling should drive by his teammate and get as close as possible. When that happens the defensive player is forced to either run into the teammate or stop and try to move around him. That act of stopping or blocking the defensive player is called the pick.

Utah's John Stockton and Karl Malone are masters of the pick and roll.

Once the defensive player makes contact with the player setting the pick, the player setting the pick should spin on the foot farthest from the basket and move toward it. The defensive player guarding the player who set the pick will most likely switch over to the player dribbling. If that happens, then the player rolling to the basket will be wide open.

If the defender guarding the player picking does not step

out and guard the dribbler, then the dribbler can either drive to the basket or take an open jump shot. Either way, the first defender will have a very difficult time catching up with the play since he will have been stopped or at least delayed by the pick.

You should practice this play every day with different teammates. Remember, it can be used anywhere on the court. It is, however, most effective against teams playing man-to-man defense.

THE BACK DOOR

The second play is called the "back door." The back door play is a perfect weapon to use against overly aggressive defensive players. Once again, any two players on the court can execute the back door play. Like the pick and roll, it can be used all over the court and is best used against man-to-man defenses.

The back door works best when a defensive player is overplaying an offensive player without the ball. That means the defender is playing particularly close to the offensive player, trying to keep him from receiving a pass.

To break free and work the back door, the offensive player should take two quick steps toward the player with the ball. Just as the defensive player catches up, stop and break for the basket or into the open. If the pass is made quickly, very few defensive players are fast enough to catch up. Even if the defender does make it back, that player is usually out of position since the offensive player would now have his body between the defensive player and the ball or basket.

Run the back door on an aggressive defensive player a couple of times and that player is sure to back off and give you some room.

When setting the pick, make sure both feet are planted and your arms are in close to your body. Extending your arms out from your body when setting a pick can result in a foul. Also, you cannot move when setting the pick. You must remain set in your position until the offensive player has gone by.

If you are dribbling the ball, keep your head up. You should dribble as close to your teammate setting the pick as possible while maintaining control of the ball. The pick can only occur when the defensive player runs into the player setting the screen, or pick.

A quick decision makes the pick and roll most effective. If the play is executed correctly, the player dribbling the ball will either have an open jump shot, a clear path to the basket for a layup or an open teammate rolling to the basket. A quick decision regarding these options is important to the success of the play.

It is most important that the player dribbling the ball has the ability to use both hands without looking at the ball. By keeping your head up and your eyes on your teammates, you will be able to spot back door opportunities.

The player on the receiving end of a back door pass must be aware of the other defensive players. Breaking toward the basket without any knowledge of what's in front of you could result in a charge. Move quickly and keep your eyes on the passer, but also be aware of other defenders who can move into your path.

tips on the back door

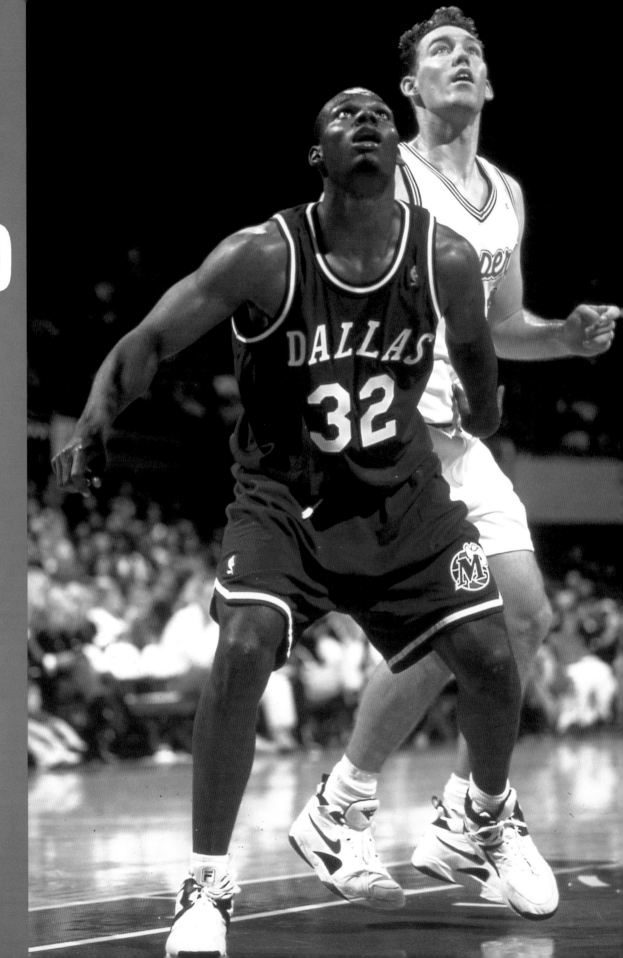

rebounding

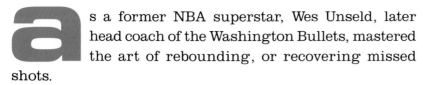s a former NBA superstar, Wes Unseld, later head coach of the Washington Bullets, mastered the art of rebounding, or recovering missed shots.

When a player from either team grabs a missed shot, he is credited with a rebound. Rebounds occur off any missed shot including free throws. That's why Unseld has a very simple rule about rebounding:

"The first thing players have to do is understand the value of thinking 'miss,'" says Unseld. "No matter where a shot is taken or who is taking that shot, you have to think that the shooter is going to miss.

"It doesn't matter if the player is a good shooter or a bad shooter. To be a great rebounder you have to be thinking about a missed shot anytime a shot is taken." Even though, at 6 foot 7½ inches, Unseld was shorter than other centers, his approach helped him become one of the game's greatest rebounders.

According to Unseld, there are four basic steps to effective rebounding. It is important to note that while it is easier for taller players or those with great jumping ability to get rebounds, any player can be a good rebounder if that player follows these steps:

1. THINK MISS   No one makes every shot. No matter who is shooting or where the shot is coming from, be prepared. Think miss. Don't forget, as great as they were, Larry Bird and Michael Jordan missed about half the shots they took.

2. BLOCK OUT YOUR MAN   There are two ways to effectively block your man from getting a rebound ahead of you. One is the "frontal step." When the man closest to you moves to grab a rebound, step in front of him and make contact. Keep yourself balanced and wide with your legs apart and your knees slightly bent.

"The benefit of the frontal step is that you are balanced and you can approach the ball quickly as it comes off the basket," says Unseld.

The other method is the "reverse pivot." A pivot is

Opposite: **Dallas forward Jamal Mashburn blocks out an opponent as he looks for a rebound.**

achieved by putting the ball of a foot on one spot. Moving around on the front part of that foot without lifting the foot is called a pivot. You can pivot with either foot.

The reverse pivot is useful when your back is to the basket. When a shot is taken, spin, or pivot, on one foot. For example, plant your right foot on the floor. When the shot goes up, turn on your right foot and bring your left leg all the way across your body so that you are now facing the basket. This allows you to get into rebounding position and still keep the offensive player behind you and away from the ball.

"The reverse pivot allows you to cover a lot of area very quickly," says Unseld. "With one step you can move to either side of the floor quickly."

Alonzo Mourning of the Charlotte Hornets battles two Lakers for a rebound.

3. APPROACH
This is the process of getting from the spot at which you are blocking out another player

Dikembe Mutombo of the Denver Nuggets grabs this rebound with both hands.

to where you think the ball is going to come off the rim. That movement must be quick. Usually, you have to move into position in one to two seconds if you hope to grab a missed shot. The best rebounders are also able to figure out the angle at which the ball will come off the rim. According to Unseld, that's not nearly as difficult as it sounds.

New York Knicks power forward Charles Oakley protects the rebound by holding it up and away from his body.

"When a shot is taken on one side of the basket, seven out of 10 times it comes off on the other side," says Unseld. "But remember, in the time it takes the ball to travel to the basket, hit the rim, bounce upward and come back down, you have to get yourself into position and block out your man."

4. THE ACTUAL REBOUND

"When you get yourself in position, or into your approach, jump up, jump wide and jump strong," Unseld advises. "Position your feet so that you are balanced and able to hold your position and go up strong.

"How high you can jump has nothing to do with being a consistently good rebounder. Great jumpers don't always make great rebounders. You have to get a solid position and go up strong."

Next, make sure you reach for the ball with both hands. Unseld suggests extending your arms to make sure you get a good, solid grip.

"As soon as your fingertips touch the ball, lock in on it," says Unseld. "Then lock your wrist and elbow and keep your shoulders strong. Come down with the ball the same way you went up for it. Keep the ball up, out and away from your body. That's important. Remember those three words: up, out, away.

"That helps prevent opponents from being able to reach around and knock the ball out of your hands. There are so many players who lose rebounds because they keep the ball too close to their body, where it's easy to reach."

wall drill

It's important to develop good hands if you hope to be a good rebounder. Take a ball and stand about five feet from a wall. With both hands bring the ball over your head and throw it against the wall as hard as possible. Each time it comes back, lock onto it as if it was a rebound. Do this while walking along the wall staying about five feet away.

When you feel comfortable catching the ball from that distance, move one step back and continue the drill. Move back as far as you can comfortably while using the proper mechanics of the drill.

Get within two feet of the wall and throw the ball with two hands from your chin. This is the part of the drill that helps develop the concentration you need to rebound with other players all around you.

If you miss the ball, it will come back and hit you in the head. So you must concentrate on catching the ball. This drill also helps you get used to controlling the ball with a strong grip.

individual drills

power drill

Practice taking the ball off the backboard using all the techniques described by Unseld.

Throw the ball off the backboard, set yourself in rebounding position with your body wide and strong. Jump into the air after the ball. At the top of your jump, grab the ball with two hands and bring it straight down, remembering to keep the ball up, out and away.

You might also bring the ball down, get yourself set and then go back up and put the ball in the basket.

**Throw the ball off
the backboard.**

**Go up strong for
the rebound with
two hands.**

Bring the ball
down and keep it
up, out and away.

Finish by going
up for a shot.

tip drill

This is a great combination drill for teams. One player starts by tipping the ball against the backboard five times. On the fifth tip, the player goes up and grabs the ball with two hands. That player comes down, turns and throws a pass to the next player in line.

The player throwing the pass then goes up and plays defense against the player with the ball. After the offensive player scores or misses a shot, he turns around, does the tip drill and throws a pass to the next person in line and then plays defense.

team drills

"go" drill

Place a ball on the floor under the hoop with five offensive and five defensive players at various spots around the basket. One person, usually the coach, hollers "Go." The defensive players turn, pivot, make contact with the offensive players and block them out. A defensive player should be able to get to the ball before any of the offensive players can.

Another version of this drill is to have five offensive and five defensive players on the floor. Another player or coach then takes a shot from about 15 feet away. The defensive players then turn, pivot, make contact, block out the offensive players and go for the rebound.

Defensive players begin by guarding the offensive players.

On "Go" the defensive players turn, pivot and block out.

Everyone then goes for the ball.

3-on-3 drill

Form three single-file lines, one starting at the middle of the free-throw line, the other two on either side of the lane about six feet from the basket. The first player in each line becomes a defender with his back to the basket. The next in line is an offensive player facing the basket.

A player or coach then takes a shot and the three defensive players must turn and block out their offensive man. After the play is finished, the offensive players take over on defense while the defensive players go to the back of their respective lines.

When the coach shoots . . .

. . . turn, pivot and block out.

Think miss.

Locate your opponent and block him out as soon as the ball goes up.

Stay balanced and keep a strong position.

Jump up, jump wide and jump strong.

Lock onto the ball with both hands.

Come down with the ball the same way you went up after it.

Keep the ball up, out and away from your body.

wes unseld's rebounding tips

ong before Don Chaney became head coach of the Detroit Pistons he established himself as one of the greatest defensive guards in NBA history. Though not as fast or quick as some of his opponents, Chaney mastered the fundamentals of individual and team defense. Along the way, Chaney found out why some players become excellent defenders and others never learn.

He also realized that playing solid defense has very little to do with speed or quickness. According to Chaney, defense comes down to hard work and awareness.

"The first big myth about playing defense is that you have to have speed and quick feet," says Chaney. "That's not true. Defense is played with anticipation, or being aware of what's going on around you, good body balance and basic fundamentals. There are certain fundamentals you have to follow. But anyone can play defense. If you are willing to work and watch what's going on around you, then you can become a solid defensive player."

Horace Grant, formerly with the Chicago Bulls, made the NBA All-Defensive Second Team during the 1993–94 season.

the set-up

Like shooting or dribbling, defense demands a proper set-up. To keep yourself balanced and ready to move, stay on the balls, or front, of your feet. Do not stand flat footed or back on your heels. If you are not up on the front of your feet and ready to move, offensive players can easily dribble by you.

Also, keep your feet as wide apart as your shoulders. If your feet are too close together, it's harder to move quickly. Bend your knees slightly with your trunk, or backside, low.

"Once you have yourself in position, defense is basically played with the hands and feet," says Chaney. "Remember, stay up on the balls of your feet with your trunk low. Extend one hand down low on the ball and the other up higher to guard against a shot or a pass."

MAN-TO-MAN   Man-to-man defense is the only kind of defense allowed in the NBA and in many youth leagues. Zone defenses, which can be used in high school and college, are illegal in the NBA. But every player, regardless of level, should master the fundamentals of man-to-man coverage.

Phoenix Suns guard Kevin Johnson is set up for defense, ready to go in any direction.

"If you learn the fundamentals of man-to-man defense," says Chaney, "then the other elements of team defense will come that much easier."

"WATCH THE WAIST"   One of the main problems younger players have when playing man-to-man defense, says Chaney, is they tend to focus on parts of the body that move. In other words, young defensive players often watch the offensive player's eyes, head and legs and sometimes even the ball.

As a result, it's easy to be faked out of position. If you watch the ball, an offensive player can fake a pass, fake a shot or even pretend to be going one way and then quickly switch. Since the offensive player knows where he's headed, it's almost impossible, even for the quickest defender, to recover in time to stop him from making his move.

The solution? Chaney recommends keeping your eyes on the offensive player's waist.

"Focus on the midsection because the only time the waist moves is when the whole body moves," Chaney advises. "The offensive player can fake all he wants, but he's not going anywhere until he moves his body—and that includes his waist. So if you watch the waist, or the middle of his body, you will be able to move when he does."

SLIDE SIDE TO SIDE   When you move, make sure to slide side to side, or laterally, without crossing your legs. You want to slide while keeping your balance with your feet as close to the width of your shoulders as possible. Don't allow your heels to come together or your feet to touch while sliding. Footwork and position are two of the most important elements to playing good defense.

"BE AWARE"   Awareness is what can turn a good defensive player into a great one. Chaney says to study the player you are playing against. Is he right-handed? Does he like to shoot jump shots? Or does he like to drive to the basket?

"We have a rule with the Pistons that players should try to guide the offensive player to his weakness," says Chaney. "If

he likes to go to the right, make him go to the left. If he likes to stop and shoot jump shots, get closer to him and make him drive."

Once again, footwork comes into play. If you are trying to make an offensive player dribble to his left, keep your left foot slightly in front of your right foot. Remember to stay balanced on the balls of your feet, but drop the right foot slightly behind the left. This will allow you to move in front of an offensive player if he tries to go to his right. It also allows you to move quickly to your right, his left, which is where you are trying to make that player go. Do just the opposite if you want the player to go to the right.

At the lower levels, right-handed players almost always feel more comfortable dribbling to their right while left-handers prefer to go to their left. Keep that in mind when playing any kind of defense, particularly the man-to-man variety.

GUARDING THE PLAYER   Defense, however, does not end when the player you are guarding shoots or passes the ball. In fact, Chaney thinks one of the best ways to play defense is to keep the player you are guarding from getting the ball. Again, there are some basic fundamentals to keep in mind when guarding a player without the ball.

"Always stay between your man and the basket," says Chaney. "And try not to turn your back to the ball."

So, if your man is on the right side of the court and the ball is on the left side of the court, drop your right foot back and raise your left hand. Don't turn completely around so your back is to the ball, but make sure your left arm is between your man and the ball. Keep your head up so you can see your man and the ball at all times. By keeping your right foot back, you will be in position to guard your man if the ball comes to him.

Chaney offers a couple of additional points on defense:

SHOT-BLOCKING   Always use the hand closest to the basket when trying to block a shot. If a player is driving toward the basket on the right side, go up with your left hand if you want to attempt a block. Do just the opposite

Shawn Bradley and Clarence Weatherspoon of Philadelphia team up to block a shot by Boston's Dino Radja.

if that same player is going in on the left side.

"The reason is simple," Chaney explains. "By using the hand closest to the basket, you don't have to come across the offensive player's body to make a block. It's very difficult to reach across the body and not commit a foul. By using the hand closest to the basket, you are also using the hand the farthest away from the offensive player's body."

SWITCHING   This occurs most often in man-to-man defense. A switch is simply two defensive players switching men to give each better defensive position.

For example, let's say your man is dribbling to the right. Another offensive player comes up and sets a pick. As your man dribbles by his teammate, you either have to knock the other player over or go around. Since you don't want to commit a foul, you are forced to go around and try to catch up with your man.

On a switch, however, your teammate, who is guarding the offensive player without the ball, simply steps out in front of your man as he goes by. Since he is now guarding the player with the ball, you drop off and take over defending the other player. That is called a switch.

"One key to an effective switch is to make sure your shoulders are even with your teammate's shoulders when the switch is made," says Chaney. "When your teammate steps out to meet the player with the ball, you shouldn't drop back until your shoulders are at the same angle. That way, the player with the ball can't suddenly turn around and get by both of you."

LOW-POST DEFENSE   The low post is the area just to the right or left of the basket on or near the free-throw lane. Taller offensive players, usually centers or forwards, set up near those spots in hopes of receiving a pass and making a move in close to the basket.

Typically the offensive player stands with his back to the basket and an arm raised waiting for a pass. The offensive player tries to keep the defensive player behind him by spreading his legs wide.

Chaney says defensive players must first try to keep that player from receiving the ball in such a dangerous position. "The No. 1 goal in that situation is to keep the offensive player from getting the pass," says Chaney. "Don't try to get in front of the player. Instead, move your body about three-

quarters of the way in front with the arm farthest from the basket in the passing lane. Once the ball is in the air, drop back behind him and get into position to play defense."

New York Knicks center Patrick Ewing is great at playing low-post defense. So too are players such as Orlando's Horace Grant and Phoenix's A.C. Green.

San Antonio's David Robinson maintains defensive position between Phoenix's Charles Barkley and the basket.

most common defenses

MAN-TO-MAN   This is the only kind of defense played in the NBA. It is also a favorite defense at the lower levels as well. In a man-to-man defense, the five defensive players are each assigned to one of the five offensive players.

Though the players might switch, each player is primarily responsible for one man.

ZONE DEFENSE   There are a number of different zone defenses. Though zone defense is against the rules in the NBA, it is very popular at the high school and college levels.

Instead of guarding a single man, each of the five defensive players is responsible for an area, or zone, on the court. The most common half-court zone defenses are as follows:

2-1-2 ZONE   This zone positions two players above the free-throw line, one player in the lane, or just below the free-throw line, and two players down low on either side of the basket. As with all zones, the goal is to double-team the ball. In other words, when an offensive player goes into a zone or area between two players, two players converge on the dribbler while the other three cover the rest of the court.

2-3 ZONE   Two players are out above the free-throw line spread apart from one another. The other three players are spread across the bottom half of the lane.

1-3-1 ZONE   One player is out front, three across the free-throw line extended and another down under the basket. The player out front tries to force the ballhandler either right or left. As that player drives to the basket, another player comes up to create a double team.

2-2-1 ZONE PRESS   This defense is used most often in a full-court situation. The defensive team sets up a full-court press, which means it starts guarding the offensive team from the minute the ball is thrown inbounds after a basket.

Again, the key is to force the offensive players into "traps," or areas where two players can apply the double team while the other three players cover the rest of the court.

sliding

One of the most common individual drills is sliding from side to side, or laterally.

Get down in the defensive position with your head up. Stand at the free-throw line facing the coach. As the coach points to the left or right, you slide in that direction. Remember to keep low, never cross your legs when sliding and keep your feet at least as far apart as your shoulders. Do not slide with your feet flat and don't let your heels touch the floor.

"This drill not only helps you work on your sliding technique, but it builds up stamina," says Don Chaney. "It's hard work, but that's what defense is all about."

sliding II

Another sliding drill involves changing directions or using a "drop step."

Start at the top of the free-throw circle with your back to the basket. Get into a good defensive position and then slide to the left corner. Once you reach the corner, spin on your left foot and slide straight across to the other side of the court. After reaching that corner, spin on your right foot and slide back up to the top of the key.

This drill not only helps you get used to changing direction, but it's a good conditioning drill as well.

individual drills

team drills

transition defense

One of Don Chaney's favorite team drills involves 10 players and focuses on transition defense. Transition defense comes into play on a fast break when one or more offensive players get ahead of the defense, resulting in an advantage for the offense. A transition occurs when the defensive team comes up with the ball and moves quickly down the court in an attempt to score. This can result in a two-on-one fast break, which means the offensive has two players going in to score with only one defender in their way.

To practice transition defense, line up five defensive players across the court even with the free-throw line facing the nearest basket. Five other players, the offensive team, line up across from those five facing the farthest basket.

The coach or another player stands behind the defensive players and throws a pass to one of the offensive players. The defensive player across from the player receiving the ball runs past that player to the closest end line. He touches the end line, then hurries back to catch up with the play.

Once the offensive player receives the pass, the offensive team breaks downcourt and tries to score. This results in five offensive players going downcourt against four defensive players. The defensive player who touched the end line must race back and catch up with the play. That player has to find an open man and quickly fill in to prevent the offensive team from getting an easy basket.

"One thing to remember in transition defense," says Chaney, "is to get ahead of the ball. Even if your man is trailing behind the player with the ball, try to run ahead and get between the ball and basket. That not only puts you in position to see your man, but it allows you to help out your teammates at the defensive end."

denying the ball

This drill helps the defensive player learn how to defend a man without the ball.

But if he does, try to keep him from scoring.

Try to keep your opponent from getting free for a pass.

A coach or player stands on top of the free-throw circle. One defensive player and one offensive player start on either side of the basket. The offensive man tries to break loose to receive the pass while the defender works to keep him from getting it.

Once the offensive player gets the ball, the defender gets in defensive position and tries to stop him from scoring. This is a good one-on-one drill for both players.

switching drill

Put four players on the floor, designating two as offensive and two as defensive. One player takes the ball and stands about seven feet beyond the free-throw line. The other offensive players stand near the free-throw line.

The defensive player out front tries to make the player with the ball drive toward the basket. If the offensive player is right-handed, the defensive player tries to make him go to his left. Either way, the defensive player wants the offensive player to drive toward the basket.

As the offensive player drives, the other defensive player steps out to stop him. This results in a switch. Once the offensive player picks up the ball or passes, the two defensive players continue playing defense.

The defensive player on the offensive player with the ball . . .

. . . forces the offensive player to the basket.

As they pass the other offensive-defensive pair . . .

. . . the second defensive player steps out to stop the dribbler.

The offensive player is shut off.

Get up on the balls, or front part, of your feet.

Keep your feet in line with your shoulders.

Keep your trunk, or backside, low.

Bend your knees slightly and never stand straight up.

Focus on the offensive player's waist.

Keep one hand down near the ball, the other up.

Never cross your legs when sliding side to side, and keep your feet from touching.

conditioning

New Jersey Nets forward Derrick Coleman gets some help stretching before the game.

good physical condition is extremely important for players at all levels. Whether it is at the high school, college or professional level, not even the greatest players can compete unless they are in excellent condition.

Before you start any training program, Chicago Bulls strength and conditioning coach Al Vermeil advises having your physical and medical condition checked by a doctor.

"You may not be aware of conditions that would make any program injurious to you," says Vermeil. "Always get a good physical exam from a qualified physician before starting."

Vermeil is the only strength and conditioning coach in professional sports who has a Super Bowl ring and NBA championship rings. Prior to working with the Bulls, Vermeil helped the San Francisco 49ers to the 1982 NFL championship.

Though his personal program, "Success Through Training," is geared to serious athletes, many of the principles can be applied to beginners as well. The key, however, is to do the exercises correctly.

According to Vermeil, successful players in every sport must improve or develop their strength and speed. For beginners, however, Vermeil suggests doing exercises that utilize your own body weight. Also, every player should get into the habit of warming up and then stretching muscles in all the major body parts before practicing or playing in a game.

WARM-UP "Your warm-up should get your body temperature up," says Vermeil. "In other words, you should build up a slight sweat. One way to do that is to jog slowly about a quarter mile to help muscles loosen."

In a gym, that means jogging slowly around the floor for up to four or five minutes. Vermeil's "Success Through Training" program suggests at least four exercises to warm up various muscle parts after the jogging. They are:

TOE-UP DRILL Point the toes up and walk on your heels. Keep the front muscle of the shin tight. This will loosen, or warm, those muscles. As with all these warm-up drills, go approximately 10 yards. Do this four times at a very comfortable pace.

After jogging do the toe-up drill.

Just walk 10 yards on your heels.

SKIPPING   To run and jump you have to be able to move your feet up and off the ground quickly. Skipping helps develop that bounce.

SIDE STEP   Similar to the defensive sliding drills. The only difference is that you should swing your arms across your body as you slide. Bring your feet close together but do not cross them as you slide.

BACKWARD RUN   As Vermeil points out, this is not simply running backward. Move backward at a slow and comfortable pace, but kick your feet up high toward your back.

stretching

Any solid conditioning program includes a well designed stretching routine. All of the stretching exercises taught by Vermeil should be done at a comfortable level. There should not be any pain or discomfort when stretching your muscles.

There are five basic stretches Vermeil suggests for all athletes. Each is designed to loosen a particular part of the body. Stretching helps reduce the risk of injury, particularly to your muscles. Vermeil says players should stretch before and after a workout, practice or game.

HAMSTRING   Lie on your back with your right leg bent slightly and your right foot on the floor. Keeping your left leg straight, bring it up into the air toward the rest of your body. Hold the leg up with your hands. Do all these stretches slowly.

Do not stretch to the point of pain or discomfort. Hold the leg in the air for 20 to 30 seconds and then change legs.

Stretching your hamstring.

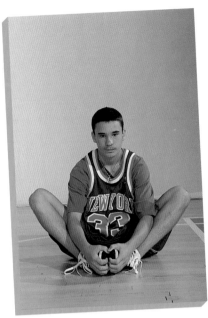 

Stretching your groin.

GROIN This is the area inside the top part of your legs. Sitting down, bend your knees outward and bring the bottoms of both feet together. Move your knees toward the ground.

QUADRICEPS These are the muscles on the front side of your legs above your knees. Get on your stomach and keep your legs spread slightly apart. Bend your right knee back. Reach back with your right hand and guide the leg toward your back. Repeat with the left leg.

CALF Facing a wall, lean forward with both hands on the wall. Put your left foot in front of your right foot with your legs about shoulder length apart. The heel of your left foot should be slightly off the ground. Keep your right foot flat to the ground and lean forward. This will stretch the calf muscle.

To stretch the Achilles tendon, the thick band that runs behind your ankle, stay in the same position and lift the heel of your right foot while bending your right knee slightly. Repeat the stretch on the left side.

JOINTS Simply rotate, or turn, your head in circles to loosen the neck muscles. With your hands on your hips, move your upper body in a circle to loosen the hip muscles. With your arms extended straight out to your sides, move them in large circles. Do the same motion with your wrists and ankles.

To loosen the muscles around your knees, move your feet about shoulder length apart. Keeping your feet on the ground, move your knees in a circular motion.

Stretching your quadriceps.

Stretching your calf muscles.

conditioning drills

Now that you have warmed up and properly stretched, it's time to either play or do some conditioning drills. Vermeil says younger players should use their body weight when doing strength-building exercises. So instead of using weights or weight-lifting machines, try these exercises. Remember to do these at a comfortable pace. As you get stronger, do the exercise longer.

PULL-UPS   You will need a bar set up in a secure position above your head and at least as wide as your shoulders.

With your palms facing your face, reach up and grab hold of the bar. Pull yourself up until your chin is even with the bar. If you have difficulty pulling yourself up, have someone help you up. Beginners should have someone lift them up. That will allow you to concentrate on bringing your body down slowly to build muscle.

PUSH-UPS   Start on your stomach with your legs slightly apart. With your arms at least shoulder length apart, push off the ground. Your heels should be pointing up with your toes balancing the rest of your body. Keep your back straight. Push up off the ground and then lower your body back down for another push-up. Do not touch the ground when you come down.

SQUATS   This exercise is designed to help build the quadriceps, or muscles on the tops of your thighs above the knee. Stand with your toes turned slightly out-

ward. Your feet should be no farther apart than your shoulders. With your hands on your hips, your weight back on your heels and your back straight, go straight down and then back up. Do this exercise slowly and keep yourself under control.

SIT-UPS   Start on your back with legs slightly apart, knees bent and feet flat on the ground. Bring your right arm across your body and put your right hand on your left shoulder. Your left arm should come across with the left hand resting on the right shoulder.

Bring your body up off the ground, leaning forward toward your knees. Do not come all the way up. Come up about one-third of the way toward your knees.

running

As for a running program, start easy and work up to longer runs. Vermeil suggests running about 40 yards at just less than full speed. Do this as many times as you can without straining. Some coaches suggest running sprints, or short 40-yard runs, one day and longer distances the next day.

"You don't want to strain when you run," says Vermeil. "When you strain you actually go slower, not faster."

By running at less than full speed you will train your body to move quickly while staying relaxed.

These are basic building blocks for an overall workout. Since players at different levels require different workouts, you should check with a coach or trainer before starting on a long-term workout routine.

Rules

To play a regulation game at any level, each team must have five players on the court. Most often each team has two guards, two forwards and one center. Coaches and substitute players are not allowed on the floor at any time while the game is being played. They can, however, come onto the court during a time-out.

Once the teams are on the court and ready to play, there are important rules that must be followed.

Golden State point guard Tim Hardaway controls the ball with his dribble.

At the high school, college and NBA level, the basic rules are the same. But some elements of those games are different. In the NBA and college games, for example, there is a shot clock for offensive possessions. In college, teams with the ball must get a shot off within 35 seconds. In the NBA the shot clock is 24 seconds. If the offensive team fails to at least hit the rim within the time allowed, then the ball is turned over to the opposing team.

The length of games varies depending upon the level of play as well. High school games are usually played in four quarters consisting of eight minutes each. College games have two 20-minute halves while NBA games consist of four 12-minute quarters. At youth levels, games sometimes consists of four six-minute quarters.

Women's basketball has its own rules variations as well. For example, the ball used in women's games is slightly smaller. At the college level, the shot clock is 30 seconds for women's games.

The size of the court is also slightly different depending upon the level. But all regulation baskets are 10 feet off the ground while the free-throw line is always 15 feet from the front of the basket.

Depending upon the level of play, from one to three referees are in charge of the game. They use whistles to stop play due to fouls or violations. They are in charge of making sure all rules are followed.

The following rules apply to regulation games at all levels:

CARRYING Players dribbling cannot handle the ball with two hands at once or turn the ball over in their hand between dribbles. To avoid being whistled for carrying, always keep your palms facing the floor when dribbling. This violation is also referred to as "palming."

CHARGING This foul occurs when an offensive player, usually with the ball, runs into a defensive player who has established proper defensive position.

DISQUALIFICATION A player can be disqualified from a game after committing five fouls at the high school and college level and six fouls at the NBA level. A player or coach can also be disqualified, or kicked out of the game, for a variety of offenses including fighting and arguing with referees.

FIVE-SECOND VIOLATION Players have five seconds to pass the ball inbounds to a teammate after taking possession.

FOUL Illegal contact between two players is called a foul. There are a number of different kinds of fouls. Some of those result in the player fouled being awarded free throws. If a player is fouled while shooting and the shot goes in, that player is awarded one free throw plus the two or three points for the basket. If the shot does not go in, then that player gets two free throws.

If the foul is non-shooting, the fouled player can be awarded a one-and-one. That player only gets a second shot if the first goes in. See "Foul Trouble" below.

Glen Rice of the Miami Heat avoids a reach-in.

FOUL TROUBLE Players or teams can be in foul trouble. Players who commit more than five fouls in high school and college or six fouls in the NBA are disqualified or eliminated from the game. Teams get in trouble if all the players' fouls add up to more than six fouls in a half. If that happens the opposing team is "in the one-and-one" and is allowed to shoot free throws for all subsequent fouls.

GOALTENDING Shots cannot be blocked on the way down toward the basket. Shots can only be blocked prior to reaching their highest point. If a ball is blocked on the way down, knocked off the rim or touched in the area immediately above the rim by a defensive player, then the offensive team is awarded two points, as if the ball had gone through the basket. If an offensive player touches the ball in any of those circumstances, then any basket made doesn't count and the defensive team takes possession of the ball.

LANE VIOLATION

When a foul shot is being taken, players cannot move into the lane for a rebound until the ball hits the rim. That is a lane violation and results in a turnover or another free throw being awarded.

OFFENSIVE FOUL

Charging, as described above, is considered an offensive foul. So is setting a "moving pick," or interfering with a defender's position or path without remaining stationary.

OUT OF BOUNDS

Anything on or outside the line that extends around the court is considered out of bounds. If a ball hits the line, then the ball is considered out of bounds. If a player from Team A last touched a ball as it goes out of bounds, then the ball is awarded to Team B. Players cannot "hide" out of bounds on offense. Nor can they run out of bounds and back

in to benefit their position for a shot attempt.

TECHNICAL FOUL

A technical foul is whistled for a variety of offenses including, but not limited to, arguing with referees, fighting, having too many players on the court, throwing the ball at another player, or kicking the ball on purpose.

TEN-SECOND LINE

The line that divides the court in half is shown as the half-court line, or the 10-second line. When moving from one end of the court toward your basket, your team has 10 seconds to get the ball across the half-court line.

THREE-SECOND RULE

No part of an offensive player can be for more than three seconds in the free-throw lane, which consists of the rectangular area from the end line to the free-throw line and 12 feet across the lane.

TRAVELING

Taking more than 1½ steps while in possession of the ball and not dribbling is considered traveling and results in the ball being turned over to the opposing team. Traveling also occurs when a player picks up his dribble and then moves or changes his pivot foot.

Glossary

Air ball: A shot that misses the rim.

Assist: A pass to a teammate that results in a basket.

Backboard: The flat surface directly behind the basket. The basket is connected to the backboard.

Baseline: Also called the end line. This line extends across both ends of the court behind the baskets.

Basket: Consists of the rim and the net.

Defense: The team without the ball.

Double team: When two players from the same team move up to guard one offensive player it is called a double team. When two players cover an offensive player in a corner it is also known as a "trap."

Dribble: The act of bouncing the ball up and down. The offensive player with the ball uses the dribble to move around the court.

Fast break: The act of moving the ball quickly downcourt by an offensive team in hopes of getting ahead of the defense to score.

Jump ball: A jump ball starts every game and occurs when a referee tosses the ball into the air between two players from opposite teams. During games a jump ball is called when two players from opposite teams gain possession of the ball at the same time. Players involved in a jump ball cannot catch or grab the ball once it is tossed into the air by an official. They must tap the ball to a teammate who can then take control.

Key: The area consisting of the foul lane and the free-throw circle.

Lane: The area running from the end line to the free-throw line and extending 12 feet across is called the lane. It is also known as the "paint."

Offense: The team with the ball.

Officials: Also called referees, they are in charge of controlling the game.

Strong side: The side of the court on which the ball is being controlled. If the ball is either passed or dribbled across court, then that side becomes the strong side.

Transition: When a team goes from offense to defense or defense to offense as the ball moves quickly upcourt.

Triple-double: When a player reaches double figures in three of five offensive categories—scoring, assists, blocked shots, steals or rebounds—he is said to have had a triple-double.

Turnover: When the offensive team loses the ball to the defensive team for any reason.

Weak side: The side of the court without the ball.

ACKNOWLEDGMENTS

Very special thanks to Carol Blazejowski of NBA Properties, Inc., whose contribution to this book is immeasurable; her flawless guidance, execution, and enthusiasm made it all come together. Thanks to Carmine Romanelli, Lou Capozzola, Marc Hersheimer, Marc Seigerman, Joe Amati and Steve Freeman of NBA Photos for creating the perfect photo shoot for our book. Thanks to their models Damir Ramdedovic, Melvin Maclin, Kimberly Lizanich, Gina Servideo, Tifannie Smith, Leslie Cheteyan, and Michael Cassidy for their patience and enthusiasm. Thanks to Alex Sachare of the NBA for his editorial contributions.

PHOTO CREDITS

All photographs in this book are from NBA Photos.

Victor Baldizon, 95

Bill Baptist, 7, 76, 112

Andrew D. Bernstein, 14, 33, 35, 42, 48, 50 top, 51, 66, 68, 82, 84, 103, 113

Nathaniel S. Butler, 8, 13, 26, 46, 53, 61, 122, back cover

Lou Capozzola, all instructional photos, plus title page, 3 top and bottom, 16, 25, 28 left, 29, 36, 38, 43, 50 bottom, 54, 86, 87, 90, 101, 106, 108

Chris Covatta, 73, 98, 103

Tim Defrisco, 3 middle, 8, 69, 70, 80, 85

Gary Dineen, 32

Brian Drake, 72

Sam Forencich, 11, 81

Greg Forwerck, 15, 75

Don Grayston, 65

Andy D. Hayt, 123

Jon Hayt, 16, 96

Layne Murdoch, 78

Norm Perdue, 27

Jeff Reinking, 34

Martha Jayne Stanton, 62

Dale Tait, 4, 114

Index